SELECTED POEMS
OF AHMAD SHAMLU

شبانه

کوچه‌ها باریکن

دُکّونا

بسته‌س

خونه‌ها تاریکن

طاقا

شیکسته‌س

از صدا

افتاده

تار و کمونچه

مُرده می‌برن

کوچه به

کوچه

BORN UPON THE DARK SPEAR

SELECTED POEMS
OF AHMAD SHAMLU

Translated by

Jason Bahbak Mohaghegh

Contra Mundum Press   New York · London · Melbourne

Translation of *Born Upon the Dark Spear: Selected Poems* © 2015 Jason Bahbak Mohaghegh. The poems selected for this translation were taken from the original Farsi collection *Majmu'eh-ye Asar-e Ahmad Shamlu* [The Collected Works of Ahmad Shamlu] © 1381/2002 Zamaneh Press.

First Contra Mundum Press Edition 2015.

Library of Congress Cataloguing-in-Publication Data

Shamlu, Ahmad, 1936–

[Born Upon the Dark Spear. English.]

Born Upon the Dark Spear / Jason Bahbak Mohaghegh; translated from the original Farsi by Jason Bahbak Mohaghegh

—1st Contra Mundum Press Edition

172 pp., 6x9 in.

ISBN 9781940625164

I. Shamlu, Ahmad.
II. Title.
III. Mohaghegh, Jason Bahbak.
IV. Translator.
V. Foreword.

2015960160

TABLE OF CONTENTS

THE BRUTAL HUMANIST

T HERE ARE SOME WHO HOLD undeniable power: commanding, iconic, and spoken of only at the right times (for to say the name is to tempt a black cloud over the earth). The bare facts of Ahmad Shamlu's biography — his date and place of birth, his ideological affiliations & orientations, his literary circles and professional activities, his marriages and children, his confrontations with exile & censorship, his intimate relationship with prison, totalitarianism, and quartered allies — are perhaps useful only in setting a formidable backdrop of engagement. They are the walls against which a figure like this might pound his bruised fists, or perhaps upon which he scrawls a verse in blood. And yet, such contextual details do nothing to solve the riddle of the overriding force of his singularity as a writer and thinker, for the unruly philosophical-poetic straits contained in this work stretch far beyond the confines of what we call the social, the political, the cultural, or even the real. From sweeping existential distances, his verses engrave themselves in the backbone of a universe otherwise lost to him.

At the center of this rare poetic prism is an extreme &
often acidic subjectivity: it is not too much to speak of a lan-
guage of the unbearable here. Fathomless inscriptions that
cast their own vast shadow upon the torture-chamber, the
firing squad, the mass grave, and the chasm beyond. Without
question, Shamlu is the one true chronicler of this population
& their execution-hour, and there are many there to whom
he must pay a heavy toll. His often-vicious, often-healing
chants must successfully transport these scarred ones from
the rank of victims to martyrs (a single line is often enough
to steal them over that tall barrier). The devoured, the flesh-
torn, the resurgent: the wrongness of this perished-too-early
generation hovers above each page, gaining immortality in his
fragments. Their bloodline is his bloodline. That he did not
himself attend the final banquet of metal is incidental; it does
not mean that he escaped (he eluded nothing, not even the
nothing itself), nor should he be called anything close to a
survivor. Rather, Shamlu endured something far more costly
and malformed than whatever name might be housed by the
rigid dialectic of being and non-being: for the others' mo-
mentary sacrifice, he would reciprocate a lifelong wound, trial,
conviction, & burden (to honor the extinguished). Compul-
sive overseer of the burial-rite. His torment is like no other.

Poetic breathlessness. At times, Shamlu's language per-
forms the magical work of abstraction: it filters the dead
through an occultish, apparitional image, extends terminal-
ity into a dangerous aftermath, and allows their recurrence
as an unstoppable counter-illumination. At other times, his
language is made to perform a surgical function: it monitors
the autopsy of these fallen, collects tissue samples from their
lead-filled cadavers, and then rinses the atrocity for public
display. Whether engaged in an ethereal or dissectional prac-
tice, both outcomes are loaded with ill-fated significance.

As for his inclinations toward insurgent, outsider, &
subversive thought, for a long while Shamlu has been mis-
taken as wearing the guise of a conventional rebel: for the
record, he is not a poet of revolution. Rather, he is a poet of
interminable warfare. Revolution is political; war is existen-
tial. Revolution indulges in constant exaggerations of the past,
present, and future; war partakes of the eternal, following
the steel ring and wicked circularity of its own insatiable arc.
Revolution is framed as a collective venture (the roar of the
crowds); war needs only the solitary antagonist (one is never
more alone). Revolution runs on utopian delusion; war runs
on accursed necessity. Beyond this, one must remember that
Shamlu is destined to lose: the poet has said this already, has
shown us visions of his own red-soaked defeat — shackled,
whipped, poisoned, impaled, crucified — too many times
to ignore. And still he safeguards his militancy, the militan-
cy of a shredded or split windpipe; and still he overthrows
(the many strongholds of what dares permanence).

Rightly, much has been made of Shamlu's distinctive or-
chestration of words: some valorize his famed descent into
the profane alleys of colloquial, folkloric, and street-slang
terminologies; others admire the labyrinth of cryptic jargon
that he winds (sometimes like a noose, sometimes like a rivu-
let) across the consciousness of his exhausted reader. But it
is the chain-linked matrix they form together (between im-
mediacy & perplexity), the imbalance of the textual pendu-
lum that swings like a scythe in each extended verse, shaving
away at the boundary of the known & the unknown, which
forms the base of his versatile brilliance. Some of the selected
works here take an epic shape & others resemble something
closer to lyrical hymns, while still others traverse the bor-
ders of anthems, elegies, gothic and decadent sketches, secret
codes, cryptic aphorisms, philosophical rants, inner mono-

logues, vengeful condemnations, battle-cries, localized and cosmological threats, and even incantations. More than this, his "nocturnal" pieces situate themselves in a dank cavern of articulation somewhere close to the genres of the lullaby and the fairy tale: they are travelogues of immanent strangeness; their childlike intonations can only accentuate the ominous intent of the atmosphere, a simple rhythm masking a more complex scheme of arrhythmia at work, just as each line conspires with a thickening eeriness through which all readers become foreigners. Alchemical groundlessness. The moodscape is deceiving, for the task is deception itself.

If there is something insidious in all well-crafted multiplicities, a minor dose of evil or malice or dread, then one must reconcile this devious affective reality with Shamlu's own defiant humanistic statements. In essence, we must wonder how the poet can assert his allegiances to this uneven race (of humanity) when time and again we bear witness to his temperamental, apocalyptic side. He does fight tirelessly for this existence, without doubt, and brings an infinite gravitational force to weigh against the towering obscenity of our condition: these are his ecstatic, impassioned, heroic, and proud depictions of resistance. He builds the silos for our forsaken potentiality. And still, there are so many other places in his poetry where all we find are human cities left thrashed and devastated by a sometimes awful touch — tales of disappearance, conflagration, and absolute darkness — and so many references to hate, rage, damnation, & wrath that one scarcely believes in his devotion to some phantom-principle called mankind. Shamlu insists on his compassion for the rest (those who stayed behind), and yet he is the architect of too many hells to count.

One might conclude that this is a case of reverse lycanthropy — i.e. that Shamlu is actually more animal or monster by nature but sometimes believes or pretends that he is human (or even its extreme variation: a human god). To this degree, he is an instrument of havoc and menace who only feigns anthropomorphic turns. On the other hand, one can detect precisely how his surface-humanism in fact works as an alibi for the perfect crime: that is, the traceless annihilation of existence. It is a discursive contraption through which the human reader is led to the radical edge of possibility, stares into the gaping beyond, and is told to undergo a horrendous test. They invariably fail this instant; they do not rise to the event, which conveniently justifies the great punishment that the poetic subject then dispenses (entire worlds are snake-bitten, burned, drowned, frozen over, or dematerialized). Shamlu's fatalistic judgment therefore seals itself conceivably as a fair response to the faltering & self-betrayal of the human other (somewhere between mercy and mercilessness). Whether or not he genuinely believes in their ability for overcoming is irrelevant; it is ultimately a crucible in which most fall prey to despair, weakening, fatigue, disenchantment, or even self-destruction. The standard is too high, the separation too immense, and the project far too excruciating for completion.

As a consequence, most of the poetic artifacts included here will cross that threshold for which they become anti-mirrors. Note: This is no longer the existentialist mythology through which the self perceives its own reflection in the universal (the "I" that consolidates everything around it) but rather the self that identifies its fulfillment only in the decimation of the universal (the "I" that stands upon the despised ashes of everything around it). Cleared from sight; laid waste. Shamlu exalts himself through the forced vanishing of all else. It is on their splintered backs that he confirms his writing as a state-of-exception and thus worships the supremacy of the emergent text over the dying world.

IV

Consider the assorted stanzas, wrought from such incomparable anger: things rarely end well for anyone (including the author), though it is this very ruination of being that lends the poetic work its revenging eternality. It is the payment for a single diagram of the unforeseen, the inexorable penalty that nevertheless emits the pulsation of unwanted genius. It is the occasion of the unbound itself, a formula for the man-unbound-from-man.

Jason Bahbak Mohaghegh
2015

BORN UPON
THE DARK SPEAR

SELECTED POEMS

Twenty-Three

The naked body of the street
    had fallen across the lap of the city
and drank up
    the droplets of maturation
        from the thighs of the road
And the warm summer of its breath
intoxicated from the visions of rain-soaked willows
was dripping in love's heartbeat.

The bare street
with the pavement of its pearl teeth
    opened its mouth
so that it could suck the venom
from the pains of a single love's pleasure.

And the city wound itself around it
and gripped it tighter
in the embrace of its stirring arms.

And the sealed history of a single love
which had handed over
    its heated young girl's body
        to a congregation gathered to witness a coming-of-age
bloodied
the bed of a storyless city.

The vitalistic offshoots of death
ran across the paleness of the grooves of the city's forehead,
the bare city
      bit its lip
             in frenzied anticipation over its last great request,
the blood-covered seeds
from which the sweat of death
      had gathered in beads
           across their father's faces
stored life
      through the ready mercy of the mother
and the dark leather bags of a single sky
were full of the immense stars of sacrifice: —
one star moved
      a hundred stars,
the star of a thousand suns,
radiated
in the sky
along the prosperous horizon of death,
an overbearing death!

And still a legless girl
is made to kneel
before the grinding teeth of the enemy.

And I blast my love like a trumpet
I make my heart quiver like a red rose
I give flight to my soul like a dove
I plunge my voice like a dagger into the crystal of the sky:

"—Listen!
to the nothing-to-be-dones
of the careless, ungoverned hands of fate!
behind the bars and metal wires of aristocracy
behind silence and behind gallows
behind slanderous accusations, behind walls
behind today and the day of birth
— with its shattered black frame —
behind torment, behind negation, behind deep darkness
behind insistence, behind coarseness
behind the despair of your stubborn gods
and even, and even behind the thin skin of my heart's love,
the beauty of a single date
which surrenders the red paradise of its body's flesh
to a man whose bones are like the final layer of a structure
their kiss is a furnace and their cry a drum
and the steel pillow of their bed
is a sledgehammer."

Lips of blood! Lips of blood!
If the dagger of the enemy's hope were not short
then the pearl teeth of the street could have
kissed you once again…
And you go tell this on my behalf
to those who are addicted to injury
and who if no injury is inflicted
become alienated from their own temperament
figuring they have profited,

and to those other ones
          whose entire profit
                    derives from others' injuries

and who if they count no profit in hand place a mark
in the account of their own injury
tell them:
"Tear your hearts out!
Strangers to me,
tear your hearts out!

The prayer that you murmur
is the chronicle of the living who are dead
and for whom in that time
     when they were alive
no living rooster
     would sing in the heart of their village ...
Tear your hearts out, for in the chest of our history
the butterfly of the bodiless legs of a young girl
will flail in the place of your collective heart!
And this is it, this is the world at whose center
it has kept you in its own tightness
     like the grain of a raisin
          to transform you into vinegar.
Let it bring lightning, this wide and nail-filled boot of mine!"

But you!
You go wash your heart
in the purity of the crystal goblet of some rainfall,
so that you will know
     in what way
         they
danced upon graves for which beneath every one of their toes
a mouth was gaping
in the eruption of their maturity,
in what way they trampled
     upon the pavement of spite

and how their appetite for bravery
at the banquet of a presaged death
devoured the sizzling meats of bullets
in the teeth of their gears ...

Prepare your heart like a recording device
so that I might sing my anthem:
the anthem of the pressed guts of the orange
in the dank air of the prison ...
in the burning air of torture ...
in the air of the suffocation of the hanging-place,
and which has not yet vomited the bloody names
in the pain-coated fever of confession

The anthem of the sea's offspring who
have knelt along the coastline of the encounter
without falling to their knees
and who died
without dying!

But you — o warm exhalations of the earth who roast the
seeds of tomorrow
in the dirt of yesterday! —
If you do not tear apart the sails of the enemy's hope
you will have dragged the history of his capsized boat ashore!

You who with the blood of loves, faiths
　　　with the blood of vast resemblances
　　　with the blood of plaster heads in hats of steel
　　　with the blood of the springs of an ocean
　　　with the blood of immanent futilities
　　　with the blood of those who search out humanity
　　　with the blood of those who chew upon humanity,

you have signed the prologue of our history
in the grand square,

we mix our bloodlines
at tomorrow's meeting
in order to serve a chalice of death's wine to the enemy
to the health of a coming-of-age that drank down
the thighs of the road
for the mother's stockpiled history of a single mercy
amidst the immense stars of sacrifice,
on the twenty-third of Tir[1]
the twenty-third…

Mist

The desert, all throughout, is enveloped in mist.
The village lanterns are hidden
A warm wave runs through the desert's blood
The desert, fatigued
           close-lipped
                 breath-shortened[2]
                 in the warm delirium of the mist,
sweat spills slowly from every pore.
"The desert all throughout is enveloped in mist," (the wayfarer
says to himself).
"The village dogs are still."
"Concealed beneath a mystic's cloak of mist, I will reach home.
Gol Ku does not know. She will see me suddenly at the
doorstep, in her eye a teardrop and on her lips a smile, and she
will say:

'The desert all throughout is enveloped in mist ... I thought to
myself that if the mist stayed like this until dawn, then daring
men would return from their secret hideouts to visit their dear
ones.'

The desert
        all throughout
                is enveloped in mist.

8

The village lanterns are hidden, a warm wave runs
through the desert's blood.
The desert — fatigued close-lipped breath-shortened in the
warm delirium of mist spills sweat from every pore.

Fog

There is no fearing the howl of my storm's demon
and no misery from my thunder's uproar
I will not give a poor death for anything.

I am steadfast like a firmly-rooted tree
Tell the homeless vines:
do not bind yourself to my arms and legs in vain.

Poverty is not the mother of my anguish:
rather it is a fragrance, smoking for years in the incense-burner

Nor does this anguish stem from the maledictions of the unkind:
rather a long while has passed since I've grown deaf to such babblings!

Instead it comes from the ocean where birds soar
over bridges, rooftops, swamps —
and after which I chase barefoot.
At that time when they become hidden on the other side
of the horizon
still I go searching for their pure mass,
my tears throw a noose around my eyes
even though in hardship I am like iron…

Or whether in the corner of solitude, I
a small bird of night emits a wail
from the farthermost parts of the night,
an oasis of torment, I
it closes around me like my own shirt.

Yet also from the running of fingers upon the curtain
and from the alluring din of chimes
and from the ringing silence of the fields
and from the impatient call-to-prayer of the rooster
and from the drifting of mist across the grove
and from the clamor of the ravens
and from the snow-covered dusk —
my heart sheds tears.

Although I am deaf to the commotion of the storms
and the onslaught of winds brings me no fright,
although like steel I am headstrong in combat
and just the same my conviction born of steel —
if a bird cries out from the farthermost parts of the night
tears of tenderness pour from my eyes.

The Hour of Execution

In the door's lock a key turned

A smile trembled on his lips
like the image of water dancing along the ceiling
from the reflection of the shining sun

In the door's lock a key turned

Outside
the carefree color of daybreak
moved like a wayward note turning and turning upon the holes
of the flute
in search of its home

In the door's lock a key turned
A smile danced on his lips
like the image of water dancing along the ceiling
from the reflection of the shining sun

In the door's lock
a key turned.

Curse

Throughout the entire night, there is no light
Throughout the entire city,
there is not a single scream.

Oh fearsome, night-allied, darkness-craving gods!
Wait until I hang the devil's lantern
from the porch of every hidden torture-chamber
of this oppressive paradise,
wait until I curse
these ceaseless, everlasting, spellbound nights of yours
with the even more eternal brightness of a hundred thousand suns —
Do not open the door of your darkness-cultivating, rotten heaven to me!

Throughout the entire night, there is no light
Throughout the entire day,
there is not a single scream.

Like the starless nights, my heart is alone.
So as to keep them from knowing what makes me burn,
my tongue remains proudly tied in my mouth.
My path is visible.
My legs are drained.
I am like the worn-out hero who sings
ancient anthems of old conquests.

With his broken body,
    alone
a pain-filled scar remains in place from the sword,
and a harrowing pain from rage:
Tears gush from the bloody eyes of this legend of pain;
Blood-filled rage dries the tears from the eye.
He is alone in his own morningless night.

Curving from within himself,
in a wasteland in whose every direction
there is a dread stored-in-ambush
pained and enraged from the agony of his own scars and pride,
he screams:

"Throughout the entire night, there is no light
Throughout the entire night,
there is not a single scream …

Oh darkness-thrilled gods!
May we be forever deprived
of your rotten heaven!
Wait until I hang the devil's lantern
from the porch of every hidden torture-chamber
of this oppressive paradise!

Wait until I curse your spellbound nights
with the even more eternal brightness
of a hundred thousand suns!"

Nocturnal

If the night is meaninglessly beautiful
then for what is it beautiful
    the night
for whom is it beautiful? —

The night and
    the uncurving river of stars
that flows coldly.

And the long-braided mourners
    on both sides of the riverbank
amidst the breath-taking elegy of the toads
                        are grieving
over the recollection of which memory
all the while each dawn
is perforated
by the sound of an ensemble of twelve bullets?

If the night is meaninglessly beautiful
then for what is it beautiful
    the night
for whom is it beautiful? —

Of Your Uncles...

Not for the sake of the sun, not for the sake of the epic
For the sake of the shadow of their small rooftop
For the sake of a song,
smaller even than your hands

Not for the sake of the jungles, not for the sake of the ocean
For the sake of one leaf
For the sake of one droplet,
lighter even than your eyes

Not for the sake of walls — for the sake of a hurdle of twigs
Not for the sake of all humanity — for the sake of their
enemy's newborn child perhaps
Not for the sake of the world — for the sake of your house
For the sake of your small certainty
that an individual is a world

For the sake of a wish that I might be in your presence
for just a moment
For the sake of your small hands within my large hands
and my large lips
upon your innocent cheeks.

For the sake of a swallow that takes to the wind,
when you cry out in childish delight
For the sake of the dew gathered upon the leaves,
when you are sleeping
For the sake of a smile,
when you see me at your side

For the sake of an anthem,
For the sake of a story on the coldest of nights,
the darkest of nights
For the sake of your dolls, not for the sake of great men
For the sake of that stone walkway that leads me to you,
not for the sake of the vast and remote highways

For the sake of a pipe, when it is dripping
For the sake of the small hives and the wasps
For the sake of the white chandelier of clouds
amidst a great calm sky

For your sake,
For the sake of all things small and pure fallen upon the earth
Remember this
I am speaking of your uncles
I am speaking of Morteza.

Alone...

Now they carry me to the sacrificial altar
Listen, all of you, who sit beholding the spectacle
For when counted, your idiocies far exceed my uncommitted sins!

—With you I have never shared any bond.

Your heavenly wish, which was to drag me across the hellish fever
of an inconclusive waiting, will turn to ashes; that I might take
a souvenir of such grand fire from your awful hell, whose flare
will make the poor hell-dwellers swallow down their blazing
environment like some refreshing drink.

For anything that is aligned with you, anything that has shared
a bond with you, I damn:
Upon my children
and upon my father
On your rank breast and
on those hands of yours that squeezed my hand
in such great deceit.
On your wrath and on your kindness
and on my own self
that unwanted, bears an outward physical resemblance
to your bodies.

I am in terror from both near and far.
Your gods would grant forgiveness to the tyrant Sisyphus
but I am the defeated Prometheus
from whose wounded liver
I have spread a feast for fateless crows.

My pride rests in my eternal pain
such that, in your every greeting and praise, I feel
the beak of a vulture in the vicinity of my liver.

The sting of a lance across the torn slit of my liver would have
been more intoxicating than a kiss from your lips, for from your
lips I have never heard anything spoken other than dishonesty.

And a thorn in the pupil of my eyes would have been more
pleasurable than your buyer's look, for nowhere was your look
toward me anything but that of a master toward his slave…

To your men, I prefer murderers
To your women, I prefer prostitutes.
In the wake of a God who would open the doors of his paradise
to your kind,
I would be happier with eternal damnation.
Sitting among the virtuous and sleeping among untouched girls,
in such a paradise: let this be your cheap gift!

I am the defeated Prometheus
from whose wounded liver has spread an everlasting feast
for fateless crows.
Listen, all of you who sit beholding
the spectacle of this stranger's sacrifice that is I — :
With you I have never shared any bond.

Behind the Wall

How it burns, the bitterness of this confession,
that a man hostile and furious
behind the stone walls of beating legends,
pained and feverish, has fallen to his knees. —

A man who at night, every night, amidst the jagged stones,
would carve out flowers
And who now
throws his heavy sledgehammer to the wayside
so as to give his hands, devoid of love and hope and future,
a command:

"Cut short this nonsense, for its persistence is depressing
like some foolish discussion about nothing going nowhere…
Cut short this chronic storytelling that each night, by comparison,
gathers at the bottom like the black slime of a marsh!"

I was gnawed upon
And alas, within the teeth of such ferocities
And a thousand regrets for this, that I willingly withstood
the torment of their gnawing
For I was thinking in this vein, that in this year of famine
I would make a meal from my own body's flesh
for the hungry companions.

And to this torment I became enlivened
And this vitality was nothing more than a deception;

Or it was a submergence in the swampland of my noble nature
Or an opportunity extended to the mercilessness
of the devious ones.
And these companions were nothing more than enemies
were nothing more than falsifiers.

I was the workman of my own death
And ah, how regrettable, for I enjoyed life!

Was my struggling entirely for that,
to make the bell-toll of my own death even louder?

I did not fly
I only flapped my wings!

Behind the stone walls of my epics
all my suns have set into dusk.
On this side of the wall, a man is alone
with his unstriving sledgehammer,
he stares at his own hands
and his hands are devoid of hope and love and future.

On this side of the wall, a hollow universe, a motionless and
uncreeping universe, spreads out for all eternity
A calm cradle, in which darkness fluctuates from one galaxy to
another galaxy, filling the cold void with the extract of death
And behind his proud epics
       a solitary man
              weeps for his own cadaver.

In the Far Distance

In the far distance, there is a fire though without smoke
Along the gaping shore of the cold sea of night
it glistens full of flames.

What has happened?
Is it a towering palace that burns?
Or a harvest stack — that has been left behind in rancor
amidst the fire of discord — ?

Nothing has happened here!
In the far distance, there is a fire though without smoke
which blazes on the gaping shore of night;
and here, beside us, it is a night of terror
our mouths warm
and well-informed of the situation.
It is a grudge that, with whatever stands before it,
turns the black-surfaced thing
even blacker.

Yes! Around this way
nothing has happened:
In the far distance, there is a fire though without smoke
And this smoked-out place is not the consequence
of a single light!

On the Stone Walkway

The unacquainted companions
like burnt-out constellations
collapsed cold in such numbers upon the unlit earth
that one would say
      hence
           the earth
              for all time
                  remained a starless night.
And then
    I
      who was
the owl of the silence of his own pain's dark nest
placed to one side
the ghastly, string-severed harp
I raised the lantern and went out into the thoroughfare
I searched among the street of people
with this outcry upon my ember-spattered lips:
    "Hey!
Look from behind the glass windows at the street!
See the blood upon the stone walkway!...
You might think it is the blood of daybreak
upon the stone walkway,
that it's the heart of the sun that throbs this way
in its droplets..."

A rushing wind passed by
the dirt-sleeping ones,
it overturned the deserted nests of the raven
from the naked branch of the garden's aged fig tree ...

"The sun is alive!
In this pitch-black night (whose black-surfaced obsidian
      has turned its entire spirit head-to-toe into a mouth
      so that it can chew on hatred's rubber)
I have heard
the hardened song of the sun's heartbeat
clearer
madder
with harsher blows than ever before ...
Look from behind the glass windows at the street!

From behind the glass windows,
look upon the street!

From behind the glass windows ..."

The first new leaves of the sun
have grown across the ivy of the ancient garden's door
The playful lanterns of the stars
have been hanged upon the terrace of the sun's passageway ...

I returned from the road,
my whole spirit in anticipation
my whole heart pounding.
The ghastly, string-severed harp
      I restrung
Beneath the windows
      I sat down

And through the melody
         that I sung impassioned
the goblets of the cold lips of the martyrs of the street
with the drunken laugh of conquest
I shattered:

"Hey!
You might think it is the blood of daybreak
upon the stone walkway,
that it's the heart of the sun that throbs this way
in its droplets ..."

Look from behind the glass windows at the street!
See the blood upon the stone walkway!
See
the blood upon the stone walkway!
The blood
upon the stone walkway ..."

The Penalty

Here there are four prisons
In each prison several tunnels, in each tunnel several quarters,
in each quarter
several men in chains...

Among these chained, one body, in the dark fever of accusation,
murdered his wife
with the blow of a dagger.
Among these men, one, in the afternoon of the burning summer,
moistened the bread of his children
with the blood of the hardened, greedy-toothed bread-seller.

Among these, a few in the privacy of one gutter-like day
sat in the path of the money-lender
Those who in the silence of the street would jump
from short walls upon rooftops
Those who at midnight, in fresh graves, would break
the golden teeth of the dead.

But I have killed no one upon a dark and storm-filled night
But I have not tied a path to that of the money-lender
But I at midnight have not jumped from rooftop to rooftop.

Here there are four prisons
In each prison several tunnels, in each tunnel several quarters,
in each quarter
several men in chains...

Among these chained there are men who love women's corpses.
Among these chained there are men whose dreams each night are
of hearing a woman scream from her depths in the fear of death.

But I uncover no such thing in women — if I were to find
that kindred soul one day suddenly...
Silence —
No, I...in the aerial core of my own dreams nothing is heard
but the cold echo of the bitter song
of these desert weeds that grow, and rot, and wither, and fall.
If only I did not have these shackles, perhaps Daybreak,
I could have passed over
the remote and sliding memory of the cold, lowly dirt
of this level...

This is the crime!
This is the crime!

Sketch

The night
    bloody-throated
        has cried out
            a long while.
The ocean
    is seated coldly.
One branch
    in the blackness of the forest
        towards light
screams.

Poverty

I have tired from an agony not my own
I have sat upon an earth not my own

I have existed with a name not my own
I have wept from a pain not my own

I have extracted life from a pleasure not my own
I have entrusted life to a death not my own.

A Scream

There is no greater wish left for me
than to ascend in search of a forsaken scream.

In the company of a shattered lantern
or without its company,
anywhere in this land
or anywhere in this sky.

A scream that one midnight
emanated from some unknown necessity,
unfamiliar to my existence
and fled toward an invisible sky...

Oh, all you gates of the universe!
Aid me
in the recovery of my forsaken scream!

Nocturnal

Dim-lit night
wakeful night
overflowing night
the most beautiful night to die.

One could say that the sky, from the brilliance of its stars,
has handed me a dagger.

Night
immanent night
        in its totality
remains sleepless before the epic of its sea of instigations.

The vacant sea
the depleted sea ...

Midnight

The cold claw of the wind has no harm in mind
And yet I am distraught:
You might say that like a black-clothed noblewoman
the catastrophe
      in advance
weeps along the roof of the house.

And the uncaring claw of the wind
in this empty satchel
is in pursuit of something.

Street

An inexorable corridor
                situated between two walls,
and an isolation
            that with heaviness
like a cane-holding elder
                passes through
                        the corridor of silence.
And then
the sunlight
and a fractured shadow,
anxious and
fractured.

The houses
houses upon houses.
A people,
and a cry from above:

—The chessboard city!
    The chessboard city!

Two walls
and the corridor of silence.
And then
a shadow that speaks continually of the downfall of the sun.

A people,
and a cry from the depths:
—We are not pieces!
　We are not pieces!

Petition

From all vantages,
from the four directions,
from that vantage where the early morning mist appears
  agile and mercurial
and even from that other vantage where nothing is
no panting drought of the wasteland
no tree and no curtain of illusion from the gods' damnation, —
from the four directions
the escape route is blocked.

The duration of time
with my own chain-piece
   I measure
And the weight of the sun
with the black sphere of the shackle
   I configure within two scale-pans
And existence
in this unavailing strait
   passes with such idleness!

The judge of the predestined
has done an injustice to me.
Who will mediate between us?

I have damned all gods
just as they have done to me.
And in that prison from which there is no hope of flight
amid malevolent thoughts
      I have been innocent!

Garden of the Mirror

A light in my hand
a light across from me
I go to war with blackness.

The cradles of exhaustion
            have halted
                        the back-and-forth of their rocking,
and a sun from the depths
illuminates galaxies turned ash-grey.
Subversive blasts of the lightning —
all the while hail
            in the hyperactive womb of the cloud
                        is conceived.
And the imperceptible hurt of the vine —
as small, unripe grapes
sprout at the outer end of its long, coiling boughs.

My scream was aimed entirely at the evasion of hurt
for I would, in the most appalling of nights, seek out the sun
with a disheartened prayer.

You have come from the suns, have come from the daybreaks
you have come from the mirrors and from the silken cloths.

In an abyss without God or fire, I sought out your gaze and your
confidence with a disheartened prayer.
A serious matter
in the breach between two perishings
in the void between two solitudes —
(your gaze and your confidence is of this caliber!)

Your delirium is merciless and exalted
your breath within my bare hands is rhapsody and greenness

I arise!

A light in my hand
a light in my heart
I polish the rust off my soul
and place a mirror across from your mirror
so as to create an eternity of you.

Between Staying and Going

Between staying and going we told a story
that passed openly into the fold of symbolism.
Our chance rested on nothing more than this tight endowment
and, regrettably
we spent all our funds in payment of this story.

There is Nothing to be Said...

What should I say? There is nothing to be said.

It blows from the height of anticipation, a breeze,
and yet, until a murmur plays
across the entire barren desert
        there will be no elm trees along its path.

What should I say? There is nothing to be said.

From behind slammed doors
the night full of daggers and enemies
                rests
conspicuously muted.

The rooftops
            beneath the pressure of night
                        cave inward
The street
        from the coming and going of the unyielding, evil-eyed night
                has grown weary.

What should I say? There is nothing to be said.

Throughout this entire barren city,
there is no voice but that of a rat tearing at a death-shroud.

And in this darkened space
there is nothing but the lamentations of a widow.

And if a breeze does stir
      there is no elm tree
            along its path
                  to commence the whisper.

What should I say? There is nothing to be said.

Nocturnal

The one who knew, kept his mouth closed.
And the one who spoke, did not know...

Such a sorrow-drenched night it was!
And the traveler who passed in that quiet darkness
and who roused the dogs with the sound of his horse's hooves
upon the stones
without for one instant it having crossed his thoughts
that the night's descent,
        one might say
was all just a fever-dream.

Such a sorrow-drenched night it was!

Nocturnal

The streets are narrow
  the shops
    are closed,
the houses are dark
  the roofs
    toppled downward,
the sound
  has fallen
    from the tar and kamancheh [3]
they carry dead bodies
  from street to
    street.

Look!
  The dead
    will not pass
      into deathliness,
nor even
  into a life-entrusting candle
    will they pass
They resemble
  lanterns
    that even when extinguished
appearing to be without oil
  still
contain a world of oil within them.

Assembled people!
    I no longer
        have any
            patience

For "the good"
    I have no hope
        and for "the evil" no complaint.
Although
    I am at no
        distance
            from the others,
I have
    no business
        with the workings
            of this caravan!

The streets are narrow
    the shops
        are closed,
the houses are dark
    the roofs
        toppled downward,
the sound
    has fallen
        from the tar and kamancheh
they carry dead bodies
    from street to
        street …

The Inception

Timelessly, spacelessly
In estrangement
In an age not yet fulfilled —

Hence I was born amidst the woodlands of creatures and stone,
and my heart
in an abyss
began to pulsate.

I renounced the cradle of repetition
in a land without birds or spring.

My first journey was a return from the hope-eroding landscapes
of sand and thorn,
on the first untested steps of my own inexperience
without having gone far.

My first journey
was a return.

The far-off distance
was teaching no hope.
Trembling
          upon the legs of an untraveled one
                              I faced the smoldering horizon.

I realized there were no good tidings
for a mirage stood in between.

The far-off distance was teaching no hope.
I knew there were no good tidings:
This boundlessness

                was a prison so titanic

                                that the soul

from shame of frailty
in tears
        would hide itself.

On Death

Never have I dreaded death
though its hands were more brittle than banality itself.
My concern — anyhow — is entirely that of dying in a land
where a grave-digger's wages
exceed the worth of human freedom.

To search
to discover
and then
to choose of one's will
and to project the essence of oneself into a fortress —

Even if death could bring a higher price than all this
I deny, and again deny, that I have ever dreaded death.

Nocturnal

A sliver of evil in your nature
A sliver of evil in my nature
A sliver of evil in our nature ... —

And everlasting damnation descends upon the human race.

A small drain-pipe in each shelter —
no matter whether it be the private hideaway of some love —
    is enough to set the city in a cesspool.

Anthem for the One Who Left and the One Who Stayed Behind

Across the low breakwater
saturated with the salt of the sea and the blackness of nightfall
　　　we stood once more;
Thrashed
tongues bound in our mouths
disillusioned with ourselves, creeping within ourselves
pulsating within ourselves
tired
breath-sunken
　　　by the deeds of those who stayed upon the road.

In the salt-lipped darkness of the coast
we listened near and far to the relapsing syllables of the waves.
And in this instant
the shadow of the storm
　　　little by little
obscured the mirror of the night.

Amidst the proud debris of the night
a voice emerged
that was of neither bird
　　　nor ocean,
and all the while
a disturbing boat

with amorphous, mist-cloaked contours
        docked itself
which was a nightmarish combination
of a bed and a coffin.
It was all an overruling dominion and command
as if
unafraid of the volatile restlessness of the waves and tides.

It was not what one would think it to be,
a boat on the expansive sea
but rather a mountain
        formidable
                embedded in a lowland plain.
And in the heart of the tarred night
the command of the dark
was so flagrantly manifest toward it
that it was as if no trust existed between them;
and thus fluidly
        it slinked across
like a coffin
                carried on a thousand hands.

Thus
my father
        called out to the rower
with a voice infused
        of neither hope
                nor question;
it was as if
        his cry
                was not an address
                        but a reply;

and still I heard the response of the rower
distinct and scathing
amidst the backdrop of the riotous waves
like a command.

Then he set aside his tall oar
              which resembled more a scythe
                     along the floor-planks of the boat
and without looking upon us
said the following:

"Only one.
The one who is more tired."

And across the rock-cliffs of the shore
        all encircling us
                was silence and consent.

And upon its tilted bowl
ahead of time
        the shadow of the storm
                had dimmed the azure-blue glow.
There was such a vigilant calmness
        as if
                since the first day of creation
no tempting breeze had ever
        risen up
and prowled around
        the distances of these horizons.

And thus my father
cried out
        in the direction of the rower:

"Behold,
        two bodies
                are we
both hard-worn
      bruised
                for we have lain our footsteps
                   all across the uneven.
And I was in this kind of night
estranged from the dawn
(where everything in this thrown-down beach
had rebelled
      against the tall sun.)

Anyhow —
We
were informed
from the outset
of how this journey would conclude.
And this knowledge
      means the same thing
           as acquiescence,
such that we knew and
offered our necks in submission.

And with honor, nevertheless
amidst such mortifying and unwarranted combat
in resistance
      we pressured ourselves to remain long-standing
(as the high rampart of a stronghold under siege
which unwavering
      remains secure.)

So it is in this interlude
that we cannot stand to tolerate ourselves.
The territory of our exaltation
has been this same ruined beach,
and alas that
          our power and our time
were consumed by the many coarse wars
          that had arisen.
And now
much like the outcast prostitutes
          we go to bed
holding ourselves in revulsion
and loathing our own bodies.

In this ruined darkness
          no longer
can we stand to be detained."

The rower said once more:
"Only one.
The one who is more tired.
This is the instruction."

And he lifted the ragged sackcloth which had been draped
across his bony shoulders,
as if he was tormented by the fog that had swelled
along the agitated, rancid arena of the ocean.

And at this point my gaze passed through the warped fabric
of the darkness
and settled on his visage
and I saw that his eye-sockets were hollow of eye or stare

and that drops of blood
poured from the dark cavities of his eyes upon his skeletal cheeks.
And the crow that sat atop the rower's shoulder
its talons and beak
were covered in blood.

And all around us
on the low breakwater of the shore
every massive boulder
        embodied the silence of consent.

My father once again
rose to speak
this time
as if he were addressing himself:

"Dwindling
to dwindle
diminishing
diminishing from within ..."

I was astounded that a military man, hand always on the sword
        could so
strikingly pass the test and
measure the fathomed value of
the fineness of words:

And he
      henceforth
           was engaged with himself:

"Diminishing
diminishing from within
a basin
to carve out a basin within oneself
to dig a well within oneself
a well
and to enter into oneself
in search of oneself...

Yes,
            it is precisely here that
                        the disaster
                                    commences:
to enter into oneself
and wander
            in the realm of darkness.
And good fortune —
such pain
such pain
such pain
is nothing more
than another wandering
in another realm:
between the two poles of stupidity
                        and brazenness."

Then a bitter curse rose up on his tongue and he cried out:
"although in this entrapping pit there is no fated hope
of the dawn,
    for the victor of the cheap and draining wars
    the dawn
    is a dangerous thing
    and such a vast one:

to be recognized
and to be passed along on the hands and tongues,
and the masses snarling
such that ("there goes the victor
          and there the victor's commander!")
if the disgrace comes not from the masses
well then what can be done with the disgrace of oneself?

As a consequence, before the night turns toward daylight
I must
traverse this abyss of horror and distress."

And then he stepped from the boat
which was a nightmarish combination
          of a bed and a coffin
                    and
unafraid of the volatile restlessness of the waves and tides.
Thus he leaned the oar
against the water's rim
and the boat
          with fluidity
glided across the dark sea,
          fluid and agile
as if it were a coffin
                    carried on a thousand hands…

I
was left standing alone and perplexed
on the low breakwater
          all around which
every stone-ridge
          was silence and consent.

And in the darkness of this ever-thickening, mist-enveloped shore
congealed with the relapsing syllables of the waves
I sewed
my sights upon the intimidating boat
which could have been likened unto a forfeited hope
and which was seated formidably
like a mountain
                    embedded in a lowland plain
unafraid of the volatile restlessness of the waves and tides.

My father
        spoke nothing
to me
nor even
        extended a hand
                in farewell
nor even
gave a farewell look
in my direction.

It was as if he was a mountain
or a shallow rock-cliff
            on an elevated coast,
and of the two of us
the one who passed across the turbulent waters of the ocean
was not he
        but I.

And at this point I resembled a boat with disconnected anchor
conscious of its own eternal wandering,
once again of such horrifying truth that

consciousness
as a term
means the same thing as neck-offering submission
and consent.

Amidst the proud debris of the night, a voice emerged
that was of neither bird nor ocean.

And hence I felt the full burden of my race's exhaustion
upon my own sunken shoulders.

In the Struggle of Mirror and Image

In that place where adoration
          is no lyrical verse
                    but rather an epic,
everything
          on its surface level
                    will appear in reversed form:

The carceral
          is the garden of free people
and torture and flagellation and the chain
are no damage to the domain of man
          but rather a measure of his worth.

The massacre
          is sanctity and asceticism
                    and death
                    is life.
And the one who stains the gallows
with a death deserving of the immaculate ones
          will be linked
to the immortals.

In that place where adoration
          is no lyrical verse
                    but rather an epic,

everything
    on its surface level
        will appear in reversed form:

Disgrace
    is valor and
silence and endurance
    are powerlessness.

I speak of a city where in that city you are gods!

For a long while you have spoken to me harshly,
so can you stand two words from me now?
Can you stand it?

Of the Cage

At the outer edge of my gaze
      from every direction
the walls
      stand tall
the walls
      are tall as disenchantment.

Is there within each wall
      any sign of fortune
and any fortunate ones,
and any envy? —
such that the landscapes
      for this reason
            have become netlike,
and the walls and the gaze
converge at the far-off provinces of disenchantment,
and the sky
      a prison
            of crystal?

Three Anthems for the Sun (Nocturnal)

It is a long-lasting confession, the night, a long-lasting confession
It is a scream for release, the night, a scream for release
and a scream
for the rope.

The night
is a long-lasting confession.

Whether it be the first night of prison
or the last supper
  — before another sunrise
either you will recall the crossroads beyond
or purge it from your mind by hanging yourself —

It is an endless scream, the night, an endless scream
A scream of hopelessness, a scream of hope
It is a scream for release, the night, and a scream for the rope.

The night
is a long-lasting scream.

River

To deposit oneself upon the bed of fate
and with every piece of gravel
to speak a secret of discontentment:

How sweet are the murmurings of the river!

To subside upon the sharp edges of self-respect
and to plunge beneath from the pure-hearted honor of isolation
with a scream of terror before every downfall.

How magnificent is the roar of waterfalls!

And in that same vein to sit even lower than the trench's slope
and against every boulder
to raise up in defiance.

What an epic saga this river is, what an epic saga!

Elegy

They said:
    "We do not want
        we do not want
           to die!"
They said:
    "You are enemies!
        You are enemies!
           Enemies of the people!"

How simply
    and with such simplicity they spoke
And how simply
    and with such simplicity
        they killed!

And their death
was so cheap and offensive
that any struggle to continue living
in the most painful sense
    seemed absurd:
A voyage hard and bitter
    through labyrinths, curve after curve,
        turn upon turn,
           toward nothing!

They did not want
    to die
nor before being dead
    to shoulder
        the burden of disgrace.

Thus they said:
    "We do not want
        we do not want
          to die!"

And it was, one might say, a sort of chant
like horses galloping down a winding and treacherous
mountain pass
down to the plain,
carrying men with drawn swords upon their backs.
And yet once they looked upon themselves again
they held nothing in their palms
but wind. —
Nothing but wind and their own blood
For they did not want,
did not want,
did not want,
    to die.

The Instruments

That which takes my life away
       from me
let it be a curved knife, if only
or a bullet
just the same.

Let it not be poison, if only
       the poison of malice and envy
       or even the poison of hatred.

Let it not be pain-ridden, if only
       the pain of biting inquisitions
       warlike in the manner of a scorpion,
of that kind for which you must answer
       and yet have no tongue for an answer,
and therefore makes you think
that the scorpion's sting has no antidote...

That which takes my life away from me
let it be a curved knife, if only
or a bullet
just the same.

Allegory

To exist
    within a scream —
(The insurgent flight of a fountain
that cannot evade the earth
    and yet experiments with release.)
And the exaltation of dying
in the fountain of a scream —

(the ground
    pulls you toward itself
        insanely
to obtain a source of fertility;
for martyrs and insurgents
    are companions
they are the rain
    of replenishment
        and the cultivators.)

To become the rain of consecrations
    for the soil —
(The death of the fountain
is of this kind.)

Or else the earth
      from you
            will turn into a swamp
if you die like some lowly stream.

Become a scream to rain down
or else
corpses!

The Letter

In that time when the world grows dark, Father!
The mirage and the nucleus will become illuminated
before your perception.

I have seen, on your life, for a long while
how you have forgotten the day of testing entirely
You discard the weapon of the populace
such that no trace of nobility remains in the heart

You have left me in the trap of the enemy,
at the will of the enemy
with the hope that I might forsake this nobility?
But have I not said a hundred times that if I stray from the path,
my bread and light will turn to poison and sparks?

Now I am not within the chains and jail of the enemy,
for I could break the ties from my legs if I so wished:
With a shadow-touch of the hand the chains will fall from my legs,
With a shadow-touch of the hand I can remove the bolt
from the door.

I have remained out of the heights of my own conviction,
at an altitude where even the phoenix would lose its feathers.
For what pain is it if your own fingers provoke the pain?
What prison is it if you confine yourself to prison?

You have seen how skillful people retrieve pearls
from the depths of the murky waters of the vast sea.

You have also heard the story of how Alexander
searched for the river of eternal life in the darkness.
Or this same tune, that no one is given their rights and status
while remaining in their beds and mattresses.

I am not Sa'ad Salman to start wailing [4]
that a wretchedness came from all this and has enveloped me.

In that time when I was supposed to ascend in position,
it was not my fortune
So why should I now moan that I have fallen down so low?

Do you think I have forgotten the ancient tales of the past,
when we had nothing either wet or dry?
It is not that we resemble a fruitful tree
that one year lost all its fertility,
for it has been many long years that this tale of poverty
has repeated itself over and again.

Not poverty, listen as I tell you what it is so that you might know:
that an unashamed tree blooms
even in that shamelessness of the salty water,
which from the drought's embarrassment
makes fire throw itself to the dirt in dishonor!

You too are cut from our cloth, Father, do not turn your back
Do not begin the sounds of estrangement high and low-pitched.
What has happened to you, that you will not open your eyes
for fear that your golden dreams will turn to copper?
What has happened to you, that you will not make a move

for fear that you will fall from the apex of the flame
to the carpet of the ashes?
In such terror that you will plunge down
from your wooden throne,
and the gem-stones of your officer's paper-crown
will spill upon the dirt?

You who does not care for gold-threaded robes
and gold-worshipping,
why do you place the crown of self-worship upon your head?
You whose foundation is entrenched in water
and your materials broken,
why do you lay your base upon this flooded port?
You whose hands do not derive anything
from this trade but wind,
why do you believe the stories of the wind-sellers?

You are a strange tale! Have you not seen
how they throw the blade of vengeance down
upon the alleys and passageways?
Have you not seen how they have killed the glow of learning,
and set fire to books and letters at every turn?
The ground has been dyed from the blood of my friends,
so do not stare so coldly at the scarlet horizon!
Look, Father, how in the chronicle of the East,
on every page is written the anthem of a new human triumph!

In that time in Gilan when they rolled amidst dirt and blood[5]
with bravery, my companions imprisoned,
you are teaching me to disgrace myself
and write a repentance-letter to suit the desire of the enemy?

To rescue the body and chain my own soul,
placing deception over honesty?
That I would turn away — alas — from the radiant morning,
and submit myself to this transient dark evening?
To sell silken robes for forged money,
and give away my honors one by one
to purchase a donkey's saddle?

Do not bother me, on your life, with your petty counsel,
for the iron will never be heated by this fire:
You take the life-saving path of comfort, and I the field of battle.
You take the place of security and refuge, and I
the path of danger!

Let My Prison Be Without Barricades

Let my prison be without barricades
except the skin over my bones.

A barricaded wall, yes
and yet
encircling the entire world
not surrounding my life's solitude.
Ah,
the wish! The wish!

A fortification in the form of an onion skin
such that when I sit in my own seclusion and emptiness
seven gates will slam shut
on the necessity and belonging of life.

Let them be shut
Yes, let them be shut
        and shut they shall remain,
and upon every gate
seven heavy iron locks!

Ah,
the wish! The wish!

Another Season

Without it having been seen,
in the garden
it can be felt
in the maze-like design of the hostile wind
the grave despair of a leaf which
without urgency
lands upon the earth.

Upon the windowpane's glass
there is the disturbance of the dew.
The road is unclear to sight
that one might enter the interior and look upon oneself

The sun and the fire
no longer
possess any warmth or light,
that one might excavate the ember of some dream
from within
the cold ashes of the kindling.

This
is another season
the frigidity of which
from within
complicates
the distinct perception of beauty.

Blessed remain the memory of the fall
     with that
multicolored storm that it sets before one's vision!

Nor is the tinfoil brazier of the sun functioning,
     though the oven is not extinguished
          like last year:
it is I
who am
extinguished!

The matter is arranged as follows:
          that something has withered and does not burn
                    this year
     in the chest
     in my body!

Anthem for the Enlightened Man Who Went the Way of the Shadow

Satiated
      he was slender
thin and tall
like a hard message
      contained in a single word
with eyes
of inquest and
      honey
and with a face irradiated
by truth and
      wind.

A man of the whirling of water
A man of minimal words
      who was the summation of himself.

Cemetery insects stare at your corpse with distrust.
Before the lightning-bolt's wrath could turn him into cinders
he had wrenched the leather strap from the back
of the storm's bull.

To test the age-old faiths
he had ground his teeth
      on the locks of ancient barriers.

Amidst the most far-flung paths
    he roamed onward
an unanticipated journeyer
whose song was recognized by every grove and bridge.

Roads remain wakeful with the memory of your strides
for you had gone to greet the day,
although
       the dawn
              exhaled you
before the roosters
had announced the morning.

A bird flourished in its wings
a woman in her breasts
a garden in its trees.

We flourish in your stern gaze
in your haste
we flourish in your book
in the defense of your smile
       which is assurance and belief.

The ocean grows jealous over the drop
that you sipped from the well.

Nocturnal

There is no door,
no road,
no night,
no moon,
neither day nor sun
We are standing outside of time
with an embittered knife in our flank
No one speaks with anyone
for the silence speaks with a thousand tongues

We gaze upon our dead
with the vague tracing of a laugh
And await our own turn
      without any laughter!

Nocturnal

At night when the silver stream of moonlight
turns the boundless plain into a lake,
I unfold the ship-sails of my thoughts
along the trajectory of the wind

At night when no sound arises
from within the silent reed beds of the deep reservoir,
I chant my illuminated hope deliriously
like a blade-shaft of sunlight

At night when someone disenchanted sings
I wait watching from distant roads
for the searing lips of a sun
that warmly kisses my neighbor's rooftop

At night when a sadness coagulates in the garden
I listen closely from the road
for the death-coughs in the groaning of the rusted chains
upon my wrists.

Nocturnal

A man clutched at the sky,
at a time when his blood was a scream and
his mouth was closed.

A euphoria of blood
upon a blue, unbelieving face! —

The lovers
are such.

Unfold your tent
beside the night,
but if the moon rises
draw
      your sword
            from its sheathe
and set it
beside you.

Nocturnal

The large silver key
in the cold pool
　　is broken.
The dark gate
is closed.

"Solitary traveler!
With the fire of your humility
　　beneath the shadow-swarm of the willows
your eyes stare in anticipation
of which dawn?

A well-lit crescent moon
in the cold pool
　　is broken
and the silver-forged gate
with the seven locks of sorcery
is closed.

Anthem of Abraham in Fire

Amidst the bloody collapse of twilight
another kind of man can be found,
who wanted the earth green
and love deserving of the most captivating women
for this
      in his view
was not so minimal an offering
to warrant dust and stone.

Such a man! Such a man!
Who would say
that the heart's worth is
      to dwell in blood
by the seven swords of love
and that the throat deserves
      to speak
the finest names.

And this mountainous, iron-willed lion of a man,
thus infatuated
trekked across the blood-soaked field of destiny
with the heels of Achilles. —
An invincible-bodied one
      the secret of whose death
was the sadness of love
and the desolation of solitude.

"Ah, downcast Esfandiar!"[6]
Better for your eyes to be closed!"

"Was a No
        a single No
                sufficient
to establish my fate?

I
only screamed
        No!

I
        refused
                to sink down.

Such a voice was I
— a form among forms —
and I uncovered a certain meaning.

I was
And I became,
not the way a bud becomes a flower
or a root becomes an offshoot
or a seedling becomes a forest —
Yet rather in the way
that an ordinary man becomes a martyr
such that the heavens pray to him.

I was not a deprived, groveling little slave
and my route to the otherworldly paradise
was not
across the goat-trail of subjugation and self-degrading:

I deserved a God of another kind,
one worthy of a creation
that does not
    arch
        its neck
for the inevitable table-scrap.

And a God
of another kind
I created."

Alas, the mountainous, iron-willed lion of a man
    that you were
and mountain-like
before falling to the ground
unrelenting and firm
    you were already dead.
Yet neither God nor Satan —
but rather an idol composed your destiny
whom others worshipped.
An idol
    whom the others
        worshipped.

Dark Song

Against the leaden backdrop of the dawn
the rider
         stands in silence
the long mane of his horse
               unsettled by the wind.

O Lord, O Lord
riders are not supposed to stand still
while
the event is forthcoming.

Beside the scorched hedge
the young girl
         stands in silence
her thin skirt
         flailing in the wind.

O Lord, O Lord
young girls are not supposed to stay silent
while the men
sullen and tired
               grow old.

The Last Arrow in the Quiver, As They Say

The final word upon the tongue
    I executed
like the senseless blood-letting of a victim
    upon the altar
or like the blood of Siavash [7]
      (the daily blood of a sun not yet risen
      or that remains late in its appearance
      or else never to rise.)

Like a seething compulsion
the final word
    upon the tongue
      I executed.
And I stood
until its ringing echo
    in the wind
burst open
the outermost bastion on earth.

The greatest name
    (as Hafez spoke it) [8]
and the final word
    (as it is spoken by me)

just like the last breath of an innocent lamb,
that flows over the uncaring stone of the sacrificial site

And the scent of blood
passed
restlessly
in the wind.

Waning Moon

To rekindle the moon
    I climbed to the roof
with agate stone and grass and mirror.
A cold scythe passed across the sky
that banned the flight of doves.
The pines said something in a whisper
and the night watchmen frantically drew swords upon the birds.
The moon
did not rise.

A Signal

Before you
    the portraitists
        in such great number
from the mixture of their utensils
    would simulate gazelles;
or in the striations of a mountain's valley
    a herd
whose shepherd, in the twists and turns of clouds and ridges,
                                is
                       concealed;
or with such fullness and simplicity
in the picturesque mist-coated forest
they would depict a hungry deer whimpering.

You draw the lines of resemblance:
the sigh and iron and unslaked lime
smoke and lie and pain. —
For oblivion is not
    our virtue.

The silence of water
can be drought and the scream of thirst;
The silence of wheat
can be hunger and the victorious shriek of famine;
just as the silence of the sun
is absolute darkness.

And yet the silence of man is the void of universe and God:
Draw the image
of this shrieking!

Draw the image of my age
in the curvature of the lash amidst an incision-streak of hurt;
and my neighbor
alien to hope and God;
and our respect
which was converted into coins and sold away.

We had all the words of the universe at our disposal and yet
we did not articulate
that one impactful thing
for just one utterance
        one utterance was missing in the midst of it all:
— Freedom!

We did not articulate it
but you draw its image!

Still I Think About That Raven

Still
I think about that raven amidst the valleys of Yush:

that with its black scissors
over the parched yellow of the wheat-field
with a double rustle
cut a jagged arch
from the astonished paper sky,
and with the dry rasping of its throat
said something
to the nearby mountain
which then the mountains
       impulsively
beneath the sweltering sun
repeated in bewilderment
for a long while in their stony skulls.

Sometimes I ask myself
       what a raven might have to say
when at high noon
with such forceful, undiminished presence
with its incessantly mournful color
it beats its wings above the parched yellow of the wheat-field

so as to hover over the tops of several aspen trees
with such disquiet and anger
    what does it have to say
to the elder mountains
that these languid, sleep-falling hermits
throughout the summer midday
would repeat it to one another
for such a long while?

Burial Oration

The oblivious ones
are identical,
for the storm alone
        bears unrivaled children.
The identical ones
are shadow-like,
tentative
        at the outer edges of sunlight.
In the disguised figure of the living
                they are the dead.
But these others
are the daring, with hearts thrown to the sea,
who stand in protection of the fires
The alive ones
        shoulder-to-shoulder with death
                side-by-side with death
immortal even after having crossed over death
and always carrying the name
        with which they existed,
such that decay
stoops beneath the tall doorway of their memory
        ashamed and with bowed head.
Discoverers of the torrent
Humble discoverers of the hemlock

Seekers of ecstasy
    in the open mouths of volcanoes.
Sorcerers of the smile
    in the nightcap of pain
with footprints deeper than ecstasy
along the passageway of winged creatures.

They stand face-to-face with the thunder
illuminate the house
and die.

The Chasm

To be born
upon a dark spear,
like the open birth of a wound.

To navigate the unparalleled compendium of fortune
throughout
in chains.
To burn
on one's own flame
until the last ember,
on the flame of some veneration
uncovered
by slaves
in the dust of its path.
In this way
in this way crimson and seductive
to bloom upon the thorn-bush of blood
and in this way superior
for having crossed the scourge-plane of contempt
and reached the extreme limit of hatred. —

Ah, of whom am I speaking?
We, the clueless to why we live
They, the conscious of why they die.

Song of the Supreme Wish

Ah, if only the unbound would sing an anthem
small
as a bird's throat canal,
nowhere would there remain a demolished wall.

It would not require many years
                    to comprehend
that every ruin embodies the absence of Man
for Man's presence
          is regeneration.

Like a laceration
          all through life
                    dripping serum
like a laceration
          all through life
                    throbbing in a dry ache,
eyes opening to the world
          with a wail
and with a curse
          vanishing from itself, —

Such was the immense void
such was the tale of wreckage.

Ah, if only the unbound would sing an anthem
small
      even smaller
            than just one bird's throat canal!

Children of the Depths

In the city with no street, they thrive
In the decomposed web of alleys and dead ends
Coated in furnace smoke and kidnapping and jaundice
A colored frame in the pocket and a bow and arrow in the hand
    The children of the depths
    The children of the depths

With the unforgiving swamplands of fate before them
The curse of exhausted fathers behind them
The damnings of impatient mothers in their ears
With nothing of hope or tomorrow in their fists
    The children of the depths
    The children of the depths

In the wilderness with no spring, they flourish
From rootless trees, they bring fruit
    The children of the depths
    The children of the depths

With bloody larynxes they sing and amid their crumbling
they hold a tall flag in their grasp
    The Kavehs of the depths [9]
    The Kavehs of the depths

A Remoteness

Who are we and where are we,
what are we saying and what are we doing?

Is there a response?

In anticipation of a response
        we abrade our nerves
and in the echo of some damage
mountain-like
        we break upon ourselves.

A Remoteness

Stare at the universe from one end to the other
that within the soft sheets of its ruinous deep sleep
            proves foreign to itself
And gaze upon us:
            awakened,
sobered to our own agony.
Infuriated and quarrelsome
we stand guard over our own acrid desolation,
we are the grim-faced wardens of our own torment,
so that we do not default on the black frame of duty that
we have placed around it.

And stare at the universe
the universe
            amidst the unstained sheets of its deep sleep
that is so foreign to itself!

The moon passes
            at the terminus of its cold orbit.
We have remained and
the day
will not come.

A Remoteness

The gloom
    of this place
        is not in that place
The heart
    nevertheless
        palpitates in the frost of this black house.

In this unpleasant exile
there is an intense despair
that crosses the outmost boundary of endurance.

We break a hollowed almond
        in memory of the territories
and the acidity of hell
    runs through every one of our veins.

Endgame

The lovers
passed with low-hanging heads,
ashamed of their own untimely songs.

And the streets
remained without murmur or the sound of footsteps.

The soldiers
passed through in broken form,
weary
       astride emaciated horses,
and with the colorless rags of arrogance
inverted
       upon their spears.

What do you gain
       from boasting
              to the universe
when
       every speck of dust in your accursed path damns you?

What do you gain from the garden or the tree
when you have spoken to the jasmine
       while holding the sickle?

Wherever you place your steps
plants
  refuse to grow
for you
  never
have believed in the virtues of the earth and the water.

Alas! That our tale
was the faithless anthem of your soldiers
  returning
from the conquest of the prostitute's citadel.

Behold though what the infernal condemnation will make of you,
for the black-clothed mothers
— grievers of the most enchanting progeny of sun and wind —
have not yet raised their heads
  from their prayer-mats!

Morning

Lukewarm
    slothful
foul water granules of the summer rain
at five o'clock in the morning.

At the tombs of martyrs
        still
the professional preachers are sleeping.
The suspended pit of screams
    in mid-air
        is empty.
And those of rose-colored death shrouds
    unto exhaustion
        in the grave
            exchange backbones.
With skepticism
the stupidity of the rain
on the tablets of indifference
at five o'clock in the morning.

In This Dead End

They smell your mouth
so you best not have said "I love you."
They smell your heart
   These are strange times, darling.
And love
they flog
beside the beams of the road-block.

   Love must be hidden in the house's closet.

In this jagged dead-end and winding chill
the fire
  they fuel
    with the kindling of anthems and poetry.
Do not risk thinking.
   These are strange times, darling.
The one who pounds on the door at nightfall
has come to kill the lamp.

   Light must be hidden in the house's closet.

Now there are the butchers
stationed at the crossroads
with blood-stained clubs and cleavers
   These are strange times, darling.

And they surgically manipulate smiles across lips
and songs across mouths.

Joy must be hidden in the house's closet.

Canaries roasted
upon a flame of lilies and jasmine
    These are strange times, darling.
Satan drunk with victory
sits at the banquet of our mourning ritual.

God must be hidden in the house's closet.

Song of the Fellow Travelers

Where the paths diverge
        there was a castle
one brick-layer of moonlight and
one brick-layer of stone

Where the paths diverge
        there was a castle
one brick-layer of rapture and
one brick-layer of war

Where the paths diverge
        there was a castle
two brick-layers of tears and
two brick-layers of laughter

Where the paths diverge
        there was a castle
three brick-layers of jackals and
one brick-layer of birds.

Resurrection

I was the totality of the dead:
the corpses of singing birds
and those now muted,
the corpses of the most stunning beasts
of land and of water,
and the corpses of humans
good and evil.

There I was
in the past
without an anthem.
No mystery with me
no smile
no regret.

With affection
untimely
you saw me in dreams

and with you
I awoke.

Enamored

The universe is a temporary camp
              in the distance between sin and hell
The sun
       ascends likewise with a curse
and the day
is an irreparable disgrace.

Ah,
before I am drowned in tears
say something

The tree
is the sinful ignorance of the ancestors
and the breeze
       is a wicked enticement.
The fall moonlight
is a blasphemy that defiles the universe.

Say something
before I am drowned in tears
say something

Every exceptional shutter
opens onto a panoramic view of doom.
Love's
            convulsive humidity is a septic provocation
and the sky
            an overhanging asylum
that rests you in the dirt
            to weep over
                        your own fate.

Ah,
before I am drowned in tears say something,
anything.

Rivulets
pour out of coffins
and the disheveled mourners are the honor of the universe.

Do not try to sell your immaculateness to the mirror
for the vulgar ones are the neediest of all.

Do not sit in silence
            for God's sake
Before I am drowned in tears
about love
            say something!

Revolutionary Newspaper

In that time when machine-gunfire fell into syncopation
I sat across from death
— On that side of its miserly table (what should be done
and in what way?) —
I would proofread the samples of its letters.

It crossed my mind that: (So why does it not rise?
        Is there not an agreement
        that blood should
        turn
        the wheel of the printing press?)

Who Created the Universe?

— "Who created the universe?"

— "The universe,
I
created!
Who other than one with miraculous fingers like mine
would have the power of creation?

The universe
I created."

— "The universe,
in what fashion did you create it?"

— "In what fashion?"
With the childlike gift of wonder!
Who other than one with vision like mine
      (the delicate balance of an unlikely one
        at the summit of possibility)
Who else has the endurance of such a reply to this?

With a luring outstretched hand
I carved
the universe
in my own pattern."

And yet for me there is no altar,
      for my worship
          is entirely
             that of "affirmation."
There is for me no sacred book upon an altar,
      for my language
          is entirely
             that of composing "anthems of possibility."
There is no
      agreement
          between myself and the sky and earth
since with me
there is no self-indulgence at work.

I am not myself.
I speak in your language
and I pass within you.

I am a reverberating prospect in the gulf between birth and death
so that the miracle
of the possibility of entrancement
      continues to prevail.

In the Struggle with Oblivion

I am Daybreak,
ultimately tired
        from having risen to wage war with myself alone.
Still there are no wars more exhausting than this,
for before you stirrup your battle-horse
                        you are aware
that the immense shadow of the vulture with its
        spread-out wings
has enveloped the entire battlefield
and fate has buried you as a blood-stained, melted thing
and there is no longer a way out
                for you
        from defeat and death.

I am Daybreak
A citizen of average build and intelligence.
My racial lineage loops back to the vagrants of Kabol.
My first name is Arabic
        my tribal name, Turkish
                        my pen-name, Persian.
My tribal name is the great shame of history
and I do not like my first name
(only on those occasions when you call out to me
does this name become the most transfixing word of the universe
        and this sound the most downcast hymn of supplication).

Amidst a dense and unsafe night
it was into such a roadside inn that I descended
elderly and tired from the outset.

In an aggravated house they anticipated my arrival
by the drinking fountain of the mirror
near the mystics' temple
(it is thus perhaps
that I discovered the shadow of Satan
from the very beginning
stalking after me).

At five years of age
I was still troubled by the striking disbelief over my own birth
and would swagger with the grunting of a drunken camel and with
the ghostly presence of poisonous reptiles

Without roots
upon salt-ridden earth
in a badland more removed than the dust-covered memories of
the last row of palm trees
on the edge of the last dry river.

At five years of age
with the desolate tract beneath my feet
amidst a naked region of sand I ran in search of a mirage's outline
side-by-side with my sister who was still
unacquainted
with the ravishing amber of men.

The first time that, before my very eyes, I encountered that dejected,
self-whipped Abel
I was six years old.

And the ceremonies
were in harsh effect:
a single-file rank of soldiers with the silent arrangement of the
cold pawns of a chessboard,
and the grandeur of a dancing-colored flag
and the blearing of trumpets
and the chance-wasting, low beat of a drum
so that Abel would not pale from hearing himself wail throughout.

I am Daybreak
tired of warring with myself
tired of the drinking fountain and the temple and the mirage
tired of the desert and the whip and the imposition
tired of the humiliation of Abel's self-annihilation.

It is a long while that I have not unleashed this, and yet now
it is time that I let burst forth a scream
from the depths of my liver
that ultimately, here and now, it is Satan who lays hands upon me.

The single-file rank of cold pawns is arranged
and the flag
with its awful majesty of color
is unfurled.

The ceremonies are at the height
of their perfection and flawlessness
In truth, it is well-deserving of those who are behind it
in the manner of the burnt-out wick of a worthless candle
that they keep clipping down with scissors.

They have stationed me across from the cold rank
and the gold-embroidered gag is prepared
upon a tin platter
beside a handful of basil and pounded onions.

And now the lieutenant's mistress comes forward naked
with the alluring beauty-mark of the nation's brand
upon her shameful parts
and now the low beat of the drum:
thus the ceremonies commence.

It is time that I spit out the entirety of my hatred
in an endless uproar
I am the first and last Daybreak
I am Abel standing on the platform of contempt
I am the honor of the cosmos, having lashed myself
such that the black fire of my agony
leaves Hell itself, in its insignificant holdings, disgraced.

2.
In a hospital bed that resembles an island amidst the infinite
disoriented and perplexed, I dart my eyes in every direction:

This hospital is not for those with tuberculosis.
The overseers and caretakers are interwoven in a joyless
festival.
Lepers stroll around freely, with half-crushed eyelids
and two hearts in a ruptured bag
and a foul puddle of urine and red herbal seeds in the veins
as they sweep the dust from the ruins

with the spear-points of brooms.
The hallways carry the ominous feeling of some monstrous
shadow-presence who gives the command of silence
It is the axis of the dormitories with iron rings upon stone walls
and a whip and sword upon the wall.
The diarrhetics
wrest their shame, in gardens full of flowers,
onto the butcher's hook
and a fit heart beats in the operating room
in a small tub of soft mud and cotton
amidst the snoring of birds beneath the surgeon's table.

Here they recommend the leeching of healthy hearts
so that somewhat high and delirious like an intoxicated canary
you give yourself over to the tune of the sweetest melody
of your existence up until death's threshold
for you know that
tranquility
                    is roasted corn in the stomach's reed-tripe
                        which fulfills its destiny in a cage,
until the security officer places the paper slip of relief in your palm
and the pill-bottle of codeine in the pocket of your gown
— one in the morning, one at night, with love!

At present the weary night is passing
from the sanctum of boxwood
and in the kitchen
                right at this moment
the surgeon's assistant
for the breakfast of the head doctor
strips naked an unruly poet
(does anyone object?)

And in a hearse on its way to the graveyard
the officially-declared corpses
still have some straining within them
and among the pulses and the tongues still,
from the fever of rage, some pounding and fire.

Naked on the operating table, I am strapped down
and yet I must release an outcry
I am the honor of the cosmos, after all
I am Abel
and in the marrow-bowl of my cranium
is a morsel for the head doctor's late breakfast.

With a bitter howl
I will make of the morsel in his mouth a serpent's venom
I am Daybreak, after all
I am the vanguard of the sun.

Contemplation ...

Contemplation
in silence.

The one who contemplates
is compelled to tie breath downward [10]
But then when the epoch
scarred and guiltless
offers its testimony
it speaks in a thousand languages.

Interpreter of Catastrophe

What can be said of the arena
when it is barren of both player and game?
Here absolute beauty would not work
since the wallpaper would also
have to be beautiful.

Amidst the default of mankind
the universe has no identity,

amidst the default of history
art
is shameless flirtation and pain,

a closed mouth
is the deceiver's fear of exposure,

a closed hand
is the obstruction of humanity from its miracle,

spilled blood
is the throwing of reverence into the trash-heap
in exchange for a glutton's ravenous excess.

Art is a testimony that descends from sincerity:
a light that translates the catastrophe
so that mankind
might recollect its tainted integrity.

light
night-blind...
light
night-blind...

light
night-blind...
light
night-blind...

The Pitch Black of Sightlessness

The pitch black of sightlessness.
The feeling of death-generating solitude.

— What time is it? (it crosses your mind)
what day
what month
from what year of which century of which history
of which planet?

A single cough suddenly
tightening by your side.

Ah, the feeling of a release-giving light!

Lifeless Nature

A stack of paper
on the table
at the first sight of sunlight.

A cryptic book and
a burned-out cigarette beside a neglected cup of tea.

An outlawed dialogue
in the mind.

Summary of Conditions

Nothing would be left behind
        not even
a curse
        to bid me farewell on my way.

With my father's ill-timed call-to-prayer
        I came into the world
in the unclean hands of a midwife
who turned an accident
        into an ablution.

I have consumed the air
I have consumed the ocean
I have consumed the planet
I have consumed God
And as for being afflicted, in its own right,
I have left nothing behind.

For Which Corpse Does It Moan…?

For which corpse does this instrument moan?
For which hidden dead does this timeless instrument cry?
In which cave
in which history does this bowstring and cord move, this
unknowing claw?

> Let them rise, the unsmiling people
> Let them rise!

Moaning in the garden is so bitter
Moaning across a transparent stream
Moaning across the bloom's pollen is so bitter
Moaning across the tall sail of the breeze
Moaning across the high-green aspen is so bitter
Across the azure pool of fish and wind,
what is this eulogist of corrosion doing?
What is the minstrel of graveyards doing in the city
beneath the windows of innocence?

> Let them rise, the unsmiling people
> Let them rise!

Boiling with Rage ...

Boiling with rage
machine gun thrown to the ground
tooth pressed upon tooth
he took a handful of dirt with a hideous swear
and with a hideous swear
aimed it at the one opposite himself.

The trench-mates concealed their smiles.

Sohrab spoke: [11]
      "Ah! Did you see?
      Ultimately
      he too ..."

The Burning Men and Women

The burning men and women
　　　　　still
have not sung their most excruciating melodies.

Silence is overflowing
impatient silence
so overflowing it is
with expectation!

The Day After

In the final instant,
the final compassionate wise-man of existence
constructed the apparatus of the war-chariot
which turned the burnt smoke of the vehicle
and the combustive expenditure of its ammunition
into an elixir
that made the earth more fertile
and protected outer space from pollution!

Like the Pit of Shaghad ...

Like the pit of Shaghad [12]
a throat full of daggers rests in my memory:
Like the thought of a putrid swamp it comes back to mind
      the scream,
           slice by slice, falls away.

Like the Drunken-in-Heat Fountains of Fire...

Like the drunken-in-heat fountains of fire
amidst a furnace of paste
I howled in the direction of the lime moon.
Our blood-spurting trachea
The insults to the nerves
proved the transparent blasphemy of rebellion.
Such interminable hardship of living, such unreaping
hardship!
The viscosity of the blood of ongoing captivity
in the bitter arenas of the vein
        in the affectionless, stone arenas...

Do not deceive us!
Our existence was your poison,
in order to satisfy this butcher's pleasure for the kill.
Damnation and shame upon you!

The First I Saw in the World...

The first I saw in the world
I howled from exhilaration:
"I am, ah
that ultimate miracle
upon the small planet of water and green!"

But once I had existed in the world some time
I pulsed with amazement inside myself:
to be the inheritor of that unfathomable triviality
that I would see and hear with my eyes and ears!

After observing my surroundings for a while
a cry of distrust broke in my throat:
look how menacingly the razor hangs above my head
in the hand of that to which I had given unconditional trust.

And now that I leave behind this shack of the miracle
there is nothing in me but a sigh of regret:
an axe drowned in blood
upon the platform of uncertain belief and
a bloody rivulet gushing from the heights of certainty.

Jagged and Limitless ...

Jagged and limitless
in the duration of foregone times
columns of bones
vacant eye sockets
naked ribs
a mouth
      without a single scream arisen
all its teeth fallen out,
the foreign-straying hiss of a melody of forgotten epochs
in the drone of an archaic wind
    unceasing still
        from a whenever antiquity.

The wind of archaic eras in decomposed skulls
upon the infinite columns of chalk
toppled over the fine sands of a nomadic expectation.

The white notebooks of innocence
in a wooden wash-basin
on top
left stranded at the gates of the passageway:
a soiled thick thread
woven across the sack-maker's slits.

And still your thoughts
were in attendance of the culmination of my bed's procession
even before my sleep was pulled into the farthest depths.

I said behold the translations of existence
so you would not think that one is forced to take rest.

At that moment I knew
that death
      is not the end.

ENDNOTES

1. Tir is the fourth month of the Persian calendar (typically corresponding with June or July).

2. The construction "breath-shattered" or "breath-broken" here can also indicate the more informal "out-of-breath" or the shortening of breath.

3. The *tar* and the *kamancheh* are two stringed instruments prominent in classical Persian music.

4. Massoud Sa'ad Salman was an 11th-century Persian poet confined to prison for extended periods of time.

5. Gilan is an Iranian province famous for leftist resistance and rebellions, particularly the Jungle Movement from 1914–1921 and a guerilla incursion known as the Siahkal incident in 1971.

6. Esfandiar is a mythic character in Ferdowsi's *Shahnameh* (Book of Kings), a young crown prince who dies tragically in prolonged battle against the hero Rostam in a futile attempt to secure the promised throne from his father.

7. Siavash is a mythic character in Ferdowsi's *Shahnameh* (Book of Kings) who epitomizes innocence in the aftermath of his unjust execution by beheading.

8. Hafez (1325–1389) is among the most idolized and influential founders of Persian classical poetry.

9. Kaveh is a revolutionary character in Ferdowsi's *Shahnameh* (Book of Kings). He is a blacksmith who has already lost several of his children to the cannibalistic appetite of a demonically-possessed king, and thus refuses to surrender his last child. Ultimately, he places his stained leather apron upon a spear and raises it to lead an overthrow of the tyrant.

10. "To tie breath downward" or "to suppress breath" here indicates the act of silencing oneself or restraining oneself from speaking aloud.

11. Sohrab is the son of the epic hero Rostam in Ferdowsi's *Shahnameh* (Book of Kings). He perishes because of a fatal misunderstanding in hand-to-hand combat with his own father.

12. Shaghad is the evil half-brother of the epic hero Rostam from Ferdowsi's *Shahnameh* (Book of Kings). According to the story, Shaghad betrays Rostam by constructing a pit of poisoned spikes and knives and then lures him into falling to his death.

AUTHOR BIOGRAPHY

Ahmad Shamlu (1925–2000) was the most colossal, daring, and often intimidating rebel-voice of Persian "new poetry," injecting an incendiary, experimental outlook that at once subverted and enlivened the cultural landscape of his day. Following in the wake of such eminent founders of Iranian modernism as Sadeq Hedayat (1903–1951) and Nima Yushij (1896–1960), Shamlu then effectively launched contemporary Persian literature into its next phases of artistic innovation and thematic refinement, calling forward an era of vast improvisation both similar and distinct from western avant-garde trends in surrealism, minimalism, futurism, absurdism, existentialism, and even post-modernism. In the elite prism of his writing emerged a singular negotiation of modernity's crisis of representation that impacted and irreversibly transformed the Iranian national consciousness at its most profound registers. To this end, Shamlu became perhaps the most identifiable signpost of an æsthetic and intellectual renaissance thriving both before and after the Iranian Revolution of 1979, and his dynamic contributions have yielded unparalleled repercussions for the question of Middle Eastern writing and world literature at large.

Ahmad Shamlu was born in Tehran, Iran in 1925 to a father whose position as a low-level military officer compelled the family to move constantly between remote provinces.

This disrupted Shamlu's early education, never allowing him to graduate high school, while at the same time freeing him to pursue his exceptional writing talent in other less conventional venues. At a young age, he quickly became involved in the new poetry movement initiated by Nima Yushij, which aimed to undermine the traditional expressive modes of classical Persian literature and embark upon a creative era not constrained by strict rules of rhyme and meter. He studied as Nima's prime disciple for several years (though no master's son) while preparing his own first poetic works, eventually taking the pen-name "Bamdad," which can conceivably be translated as "Morning," "Dawn," or "Daybreak." Against this backdrop, Shamlu presented his third full collection titled *Fresh Air* in 1957 to mass recognition, an absolutely groundbreaking effort that intertwined colloquial, everyday language with arcane, esoteric terms and charged political and philosophical themes. More than this, it solidified his place not simply as heir to Nima's legacy, but as the indisputable leader of the new Iranian vanguard. From there, Shamlu would go on to a famed career, publishing over fifteen collections of poetry, editing numerous literary journals and magazines, compiling a multi-volume compendium of Iranian folklore, proverbs, idioms, and street-slang titled *The Book of the Alley*, delivering lectures and readings at major western universities (UCLA, UC Berkeley, Columbia University), being arrested, interrogated, or imprisoned on different occasions, withstanding censorship and the banning or confiscation of his manuscripts, winning several international awards (and nominated for the Nobel Prize in Literature in 1984), while also translating into Persian the works of such other prominent world authors as Louis Aragon, Langston Hughes, Federico Garcia Lorca, Leo

Tolstoy, and Octavio Paz. Following his death in 2000, for which thousands of black-clothed mourners gathered in the streets of different Iranian cities against the warnings of the regime, Shamlu's multiple contributions would solidify his image as a cultural giant of the modern Middle East & beyond.

With respect to Shamlu's overall poetic disposition, the 78 selected poems here reflect a synchronous yet diverse series of philosophical concepts and stylistic forms. As for the former, Shamlu's meditations penetrate into fundamental issues of doom, condemnation, suspicion, power, resistance, solitude, pain, betrayal, rage, desire, struggle, and (in)humanity. His articulations of time and space are also remarkably unique, at once reaching back into long-forgotten ancient settings while also projecting prophetically into apocalyptic and post-apocalyptic worlds. Moreover, Shamlu's often grueling depictions of the body in states of torture and deprivation (emanating from his personal experiences in certain notorious prisons) provide an entire generation of those lost in revolutionary crusades a proper martyrological account. His disquieting eloquence in this area is beyond legendary, having recorded in graphic detail the tragic consequences of political cruelty in his country for over half a century: namely, images of firing squads, mass graves, secret police raids, public executions, and grieving widows are rampant throughout his works. In this way, Shamlu embodied for many the definitive poetic interlocutor of a volatile and often catastrophic arc guiding the modern epoch, someone whose piercing insights offered a kind of significance or response (however nightmarish) to the excessive violence witnessed at every turn.

On a stylistic level, Shamlu became renowned as perhaps the most ingenious visionary of the free verse and blank verse approach to Iranian poetic narrative, but more than this, he demonstrated an expansive conviction to test the boundaries of almost every genre he could conceive. Whether the central concern is an act of storytelling, the anti-commemoration of some historical event, or the imagistic construction of an abstract idea, experience, or dreamscape, the sheer multiplicity of intellectual concerns and existential positions that Shamlu arranges time and again proves staggering. Moreover, Shamlu's unmistakable poetic method, while frequently alternating between continuous and fragmentary modes, and also between concrete and hallucinogenic descriptions, is capable of capturing an amorphous spectrum of moods, temperaments, and atmospheres like no other figure of his time.

TRANSLATOR BIOGRAPHY

Jason Bahbak Mohaghegh is a philosopher & literary-cultural theorist who teaches Comparative Literature at Babson College. His work focuses upon tracking emergent currents of experimental thought in the Middle East and the West, with particular attention to exploring the concepts of chaos, violence, illusion, silence, sectarianism, and apocalyptic writing. He has published four books to date — *The Chaotic Imagination: New Literature and Philosophy of the Middle East* (Palgrave Macmillan, 2010), *Inflictions: The Writing of Violence in the Middle East* (Continuum, 2012), *The Radical Unspoken: Silence in Middle Eastern and Western Thought* (Routledge, 2013), and *Insurgent, Poet, Mystic, Sectarian: The Four Masks of an Eastern Postmodernism* (SUNY, 2015). He is also the co-editor of a book series titled "Suspensions: Contemporary Middle Eastern & Islamicate Thought" (Bloomsbury), which is dedicated to showcasing cutting-edge movements in literature, philosophy, culture, and art across the region.

COLOPHON

BORN UPON THE DARK SPEAR: SELECTED POEMS
was typeset in InDesign CC.

The text & page numbers are set in *Adobe Jenson Pro*.
The titles are set in *IM Fell Double Pica Pro*.
The fragment in Persian is set in *DecoType Nastaliq*.

Book design & typesetting: Alessandro Segalini
Cover design: Contra Mundum Press
Image credit: Umberto Boccioni, *Head + House + Light*, 1912

BORN UPON THE DARK SPEAR: SELECTED POEMS
is published by Contra Mundum Press.
Its printer has received Chain of Custody certification from:
The Forest Stewardship Council,
The Programme for the Endorsement of Forest Certification,
& The Sustainable Forestry Initiative.

Contra Mundum Press   New York · London · Melbourne

CONTRA MUNDUM PRESS

Dedicated to the value & the indispensable importance of the individual voice, to works that test the boundaries of thought & experience.

The primary aim of Contra Mundum is to publish translations of writers who in their use of form and style are *à rebours*, or who deviate significantly from more programmatic & spurious forms of experimentation. Such writing attests to the volatile nature of modernism. Our preference is for works that have not yet been translated into English, are out of print, or are poorly translated, for writers whose thinking & æsthetics are in opposition to timely or mainstream currents of thought, value systems, or moralities. We also reprint obscure and out-of-print works we consider significant but which have been forgotten, neglected, or overshadowed.

There are many works of fundamental significance to *Weltliteratur* (*& Weltkultur*) that still remain in relative oblivion, works that alter and disrupt standard circuits of thought — these warrant being encountered by the world at large. It is our aim to render them more visible.

For the complete list of forthcoming publications, please visit our website. To be added to our mailing list, send your name and email address to: info@contramundum.net

Contra Mundum Press
P.O. Box 1326
New York, NY 10276
USA

OTHER CONTRA MUNDUM PRESS TITLES

Gilgamesh

Ghérasim Luca, *Self-Shadowing Prey*

Rainer J. Hanshe, *The Abdication*

Walter Jackson Bate, *Negative Capability*

Miklós Szentkuthy, *Marginalia on Casanova*

Fernando Pessoa, *Philosophical Essays*

Elio Petri, *Writings on Cinema & Life*

Friedrich Nietzsche, *The Greek Music Drama*

Richard Foreman, *Plays with Films*

Louis-Auguste Blanqui, *Eternity by the Stars*

Miklós Szentkuthy, *Towards the One & Only Metaphor*

Josef Winkler, *When the Time Comes*

William Wordsworth, *Fragments*

Josef Winkler, *Natura Morta*

Fernando Pessoa, *The Transformation Book*

Emilio Villa, *The Selected Poetry of Emilio Villa*

Robert Kelly, *A Voice Full of Cities*

Pier Paolo Pasolini, *The Divine Mimesis*

Miklós Szentkuthy, *Prae, Vol. 1*

Federico Fellini, *Making a Film*

Robert Musil, *Thought Flights*

Sándor Tar, *Our Street*

Lorand Gaspar, *Earth Absolute*

Josef Winkler, *The Graveyard of Bitter Oranges*

Jean-Jacques Rousseau, *Narcissus*

Ferit Edgü, *Noone*

SOME FORTHCOMING TITLES

Jean-Luc Godard, *Phrases*

Pierre Senges, *The Major Refutation*

Claude Mouchard, *Entangled, Papers!, Notes*

Lightning Source UK Ltd.
Milton Keynes UK
UKOW05f0329050117
291381UK00009B/337/P